INDIGENOUS ORIGINATED

Walking in Two Worlds

D1468757

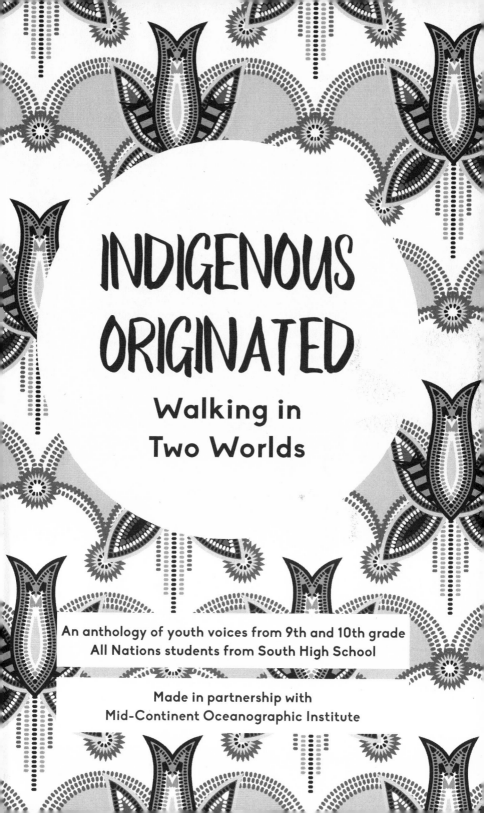

INDIGENOUS ORIGINATED

Walking in Two Worlds

An anthology of youth voices from 9th and 10th grade
All Nations students from South High School

Made in partnership with
Mid-Continent Oceanographic Institute

INDIGENOUS ORIGINATED © copyright 2019 by the authors and Mid-Continent Oceanographic Institute. All rights reserved. No part of this book may be reproduced in any form whatsoever, by photography or xerography or by any other means, by broadcast or transmission, by translation into any kind of language, nor by recording electronically or otherwise, without permission in writing from the author, except by a reviewer, who may quote brief passages in critical articles or reviews.

ISBN 13: 978-1-63489-235-3

Library of Congress Catalog Number: 2019940126
Printed in the United States of America
First Printing: 2019
23 22 21 20 19   6 5 4 3 2

Cover design by Marlena Myles
Page design and typesetting by Mayfly Design, and typeset in the Acumin Pro typeface

www.moi-msp.org

Minneapolis, MN
www.wiseink.com

To order, visit www.moi-msp.org. Reseller discounts available. All proceeds from the sales of this book help support MOI's free programs.

*"But I guess it is a NDN
thing in the sense that
I'm NDN n doing
this thing . . ."*

—Tommy Pico from "IRL"

CONTENTS

GROWTH

FAMILY

APPENDIX

FOREWORD

As I closed my eyes and asked the Creator to speak through me in this foreword, the voice in my head said to be yourself. So even though I'm a college-educated street kid completely capable of writing and speaking in my "white voice," I'm not doing that here. Simply put, the young writers, poets, storytellers, illustrators, dancers, and authors featured in this book GOT BARS.

While reading their words, I was reminded of my own time as a teen attending Minneapolis South High School. Looking back, I can't recall writing a single paper while there, so it occurs to me that these students are far more experienced writers than I was at that point in time. To think that I—literally one of the quietest kids among roughly two thousand students—would become a self-employed traveling writer, performer, and public speaker was beyond me. I can't even imagine where their bright minds and talents will take them if they continue to fight through their adversities and pursue their desires. After all, I never imagined where mine would take me.

While visiting their classrooms, I recognized a very familiar shyness in many of them, but not all of them. It was the same shyness that couldn't conceal the brilliance my high school advisors and counselors saw in me, a brilliance I often never saw in myself. I see it in them. To be more direct, when y'all inevitably read this, I SEE IT IN YOU. Part of that is because I see it in myself. Much like many of you, I was an Indigenous youth who grew up on the South side of Minneapolis. I've made mistakes and poor decisions that I regret and feel guilt for to this day. I've managed to find happiness and escape through creative outlets of expression that are dear to me. I too have battled with depression throughout various points in my life: from going through foster care to dealing with the loss of loved ones through break-up and death. I relate to y'all in these ways and many more.

So, not to be cliché, but if I can achieve many of my goals, then most definitely y'all can too. Your recognition of what brings you peace, your awareness of the quiet but noticeable segregation and separation found in your school (and the desire to heal it), your willingness to forgive yourself and others, all of these things about you inspire and amaze me. I recall a time when my mom thanked me for choosing her to be my mother. I didn't understand her at the time, but in her words was the lesson that life goes full circle from the spirit world and back. The closer we are to that light, the better teachers we are. The light never leaves us, but sometimes we become lost to it. Because you are youth, you are closer to that light. You are the world's greatest teachers. Be the light and lead us. Mi'iw.

–Paul Wenell Jr.
"Tall Paul"
2019

ACKNOWLEDGMENTS

The book you are holding marks the fourth year that Mid-Continent Oceanographic Institute has embarked on a Young Authors' Book Project. Our past adventures have included flights of futuristic fancy with fifth graders, stories of identity and culture with ninth graders, and a poetic foray into the Minnesota wilds with yet another set of fifth graders. All these projects were full of creativity and struggle and wonder.

Every year has been special. But this one has been especially so.

The 2018-2019 school year has been filled with changes for MOI. In September we moved in to our new headquarters in South Minneapolis, and shortly after we opened the Writers' Room—a drop-in student writing support center—just down the street from us inside South High School. Amidst this time of great transition, we built a partnership with Principal Ray Aponte, English teacher Laura Yost, and the rest of the All Nations team to bring YABP to two classes of ninth and tenth graders, all of whom are Native American. The All Nations program is a cohort model for Minneapolis Native

American students that provides them with culturally specific classes and opportunities.

South High is a unique place, with a huge diversity of programs and students within its walls. The goal of our Writers' Room and this year's YABP was to amplify the voices of those populations that have historically been underserved, including the All Nations students that filled this book with their memories and their dreams.

While we look back on this year with joy and pride, we can also reflect that this year was not easy. Mother Nature seemed to have it out for us, bringing snow that canceled classes and interfered with field trips. Anxieties about neighborhood violence and housing, but also celebrations about new baby siblings and basketball games, competed for our students' attention. Some of our students come from highly mobile living situations, so we saw some students leave halfway through the project. Others joined us just days before we went to press.

In spite of—or perhaps in concert with—all these outside factors, this anthology grew.

By feeding on the life-giving words of Octavia Butler, Kurt Vonnegut, Juan Rulfo, Eve Ewing, Louise and Heid Erdrich, and Black Elk—it grew. By making the publishing process more transparent to the students, so they had more investment in the project—it grew. By bringing in artists and partners who reflectively represented the students' identities—it not only grew, but thrived.

So before we thank the amazing team of adults who worked on the project, we must honor the students who imbued this book with life. Their honesty,

their trust, and their resilience are the reason this came together. These classes are full of artists. Not just writers and illustrators, but also dancers, rappers, beadworkers, singers, and more. Art and story are big influences in their lives, and they in turn influenced this book to become a magnificent creation.

To the MOI staff—Samantha Sencer-Mura, Ellen Fee, Sam Oppenheimer, and Tori Dylla—who checked over lesson plans, tallied ballots, mended cardboard forts, delivered pizza, and cheered on our students through every milestone—you are the glue that holds this book together. May the good energy and momentum that carried this project bring us to new horizons.

To our teachers Laura Yost, Audrey Spiess, and Gary Hoffert, who model radical patience and teamwork in the classroom every day—thank you for taking a leap with a new program and bringing a new partner under your wings. This book is a testament to your faith and hard work.

To our board member and volunteer Paul von Drasek, your unwavering support—whether there was a blizzard or a plan fell through—carried us to the finish line. A gentleman and a gentle man, you brought such empathy to the classroom that helped cultivate trust and community. You are so appreciated.

To our teaching artist Paul Wenell, Jr. who could turn fifty pairs of eyes away from their cell phones by telling just one story. Your honesty and your advice were invaluable to building a culture of sharing in the classroom. As a South High alum, as an artist, as a person who gives back to their community,

you helped the students see themselves more clearly. For all this and more, we are so grateful.

To Wise Ink Creative Publishing, especially Dara Beevas and Alyssa Bluhm, whose enthusiasm and frankness unlocked the mystical world of publishing for our students. To Ryan Scheife of Mayfly Design, whose expertise and patience ensured this book looked as beautiful as the souls who participated in its creation.

To Marlena Myles, who found inspiration in the doodles and marginalia of fifty underclassmen and wove those threads into a cover design that reflects the vibrance and complexity of our students. Thank you for capturing our imagination and for showing our students a new world of possibility.

To MOI's committed board of directors, our squad of volunteers and the community that continues to support us, especially for the major gifts from the Graves Foundation, the South High Foundation, the Mithun Family Foundation, and MOI's individual donors. Thank you for believing in us and bringing this wonderful book to fruition.

Mid-Continent Oceanographic Institute acknowledges the Dakota and Ojibwe peoples as the original people of the land on which we live and work.

IDENTITY

Destin Capers

Ballpoint pen and paper
2018

Where Home Lies

Lennox Lasley

I don't know where home lies.

I'm 100 percent Native,
I'm culturally connected.

I'm from a city where some people
don't got it like I do.

I'm from a place where people miss meals and risk
    it all
to have a little bit of success.

The place where dreams are broken,
and reality is turned into dreams.

Where stuff isn't handed to you,
Where you can't depend on anyone,
Where you have to work for everything.

Minneapolis

Lennox Lasley lives with his aunt, uncle, dad,
brothers, cousins, and nephews. On a Saturday, he
likes to wake up at like 10:00 a.m., eat, watch TV,
and play the game. He has lived in three different
states throughout his life.

Beat of the Drum

Aniah Smith

I am from the beat of the drum,
Dancing from dusk till dawn.

From the moment my moccasins hit the ground,
From dancing around,
I dance for the people who can't.

I get the feeling of freedom,
Of confidence and safety.

Aniah Smith is Ojibwe from the White Earth
Nation in Minnesota, although she's never been
to her reservation. She was born and raised
in Minneapolis, on the Southside. She likes to
represent her traditional ways by dancing in
powwows around the country. She grew up dancing
fancy shawl and jingle dress, but she's more focused
on the jingle dress, known as the "Healing Dress."
She hopes the future generations of her family
continue the tradition of dancing in powwows.

When she gets older, Aniah wants to become
a caseworker for the people in her community.
She says, "I'm following the steps of my mom," as
her mom is her biggest role model. Aniah wants to
help make her community a safer place to be. She
wants to be a leader so that her voice is heard.
She is very "miigwechiwendam" (thankful).

I Am a Human

Stephen Delong

I am a human with a pulse,
Who seeks solitude in the world,
And has a contained mermaid,
And lives in a walnut.

I am from South Minneapolis
I am in the ninth grade
I am from humans.
I am from loving relatives.

I am also a mixed child.
I come from a Native family.
And have lived in Minnesota my whole life.

Stephen Delong lives in South Minneapolis.

Taleah B.

Pencil on paper
2018

I Am From

Taleah B.

I am from the Southside.

I am from the Sioux,
and I am Indigenous.

I am from softball in the park, from the Pal team.
This makes me strong.

I am from the ghetto.
I learned to be independent, I stick to myself.

I am an individual,
but I get support from my community.

I am bright,
but I just don't know how to show it.

I am Native.

Taleah B. likes to sleep late or go out on
Saturdays. Her favorite sport is softball. For her
career, Taleah would someday like to be the
person that takes pictures at crime scenes.

Indigenous Strong

Ayianna Doney

I am from the Southside,

I am from the Ojibwe people,

I am from a big, fat community of Native people,

I am from a good sense of humor,

I am the famous one in my family,

I am from some white people—from places
unknown and yet undiscovered,

I am Indigenous strong!

Ayianna Doney is a tenth-grade student in the All
Nation program at South High School.

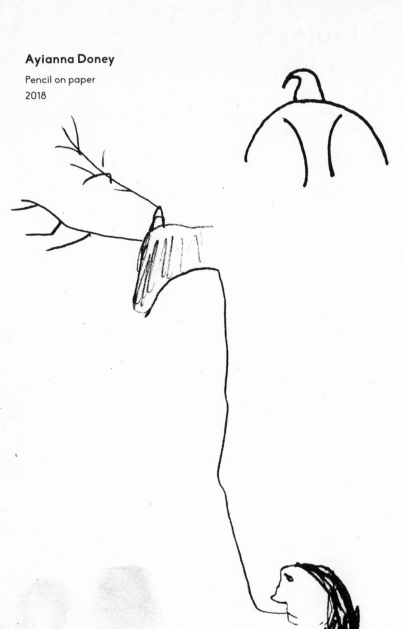

Ayianna Doney

Pencil on paper

2018

I Am

Diego Calzada-Russette

I am from the Native and Hispanic cultures,
I am from All Nations at school,
As a community.

I am from Minnesota where it's cold out,
From where it's called the ghetto.

I am from loving relatives,
Where the Southside is.

Diego Calzada-Russette is a ninth grader and
lives with his mother, sister, and auntie. He has a
dog (Gizmo) and a cat (Amina). He also likes pizza,
doesn't matter what kind.

I Am From

Travis L.

I am from All Nations.

I am from lead and rubber.

I am from common sense.

I am from lost pine needles.

I am from the wild oryza sativa.

I am from instruments and singing.

I am from bitter drinks.

I am from "just tough it out" attitude.

Travis L. is a high school student at South High. He would really like to go to the University of Minnesota after high school. His favorite food is steak because it's really good with barbeque. The pet that he owns is a small leopard gecko named Ruby.

Miner Hysteria

Travis L.
Ballpoint pen on paper
2018

Depression

Destin C.

People that you trust
can hurt you
more than people that you don't know.

Because
they know more about you,
like your weaknesses,
than others.

Because
you care for them
more.

People that you trust
can hurt you
so

You try to keep to yourself
stay independent,
be antisocial.

Don't talk to people if you don't have to,
in order to not get
hurt.

I am
guarding my pride,
my feelings.

Destin C. is a student at South High School. He lives in a house in North Minneapolis with his brother and family and snake. His favorite food is Panda Express.

Raised by Skyscrapers

Stephan

The whole Native community did this,
So I know I can do this.

And like when he says,
"Inner city raised by bright lights and skyscrapers,"
He means that he grew up in the city,
Was influenced by the city's negativity.

Got caught up in the violence and the criminal life,
Got caught up in the jam.
It got me!

Did it get you?

Stephan's favorite food is Panda Express. He likes
to hang out with friends on Saturdays. He also
likes to play video games.

A Boogie Wit Da Hoodie

JoJo Johnson
Digital illustration
2019

JoJo Johnson AKA "Chicken Nugget Boii" is a graphic
designer. He lives at home and lives in the cut, like a Band-Aid.
He lives with his mom and brother in Minneapolis.

5-Foot-2

Andrea Dorr

Yeah I'm 5'2" so I'm kinda tiny
But ain't no one really like me,
But if you trying to play with me
This might get deadly,

Yeah, you in danger,
You treating me like silver,
But my heart is made of gold,
I'm known for being bold,

I love being alone,
You wannabe
Like me,
You kinda like my clone.

Andrea Dorr lives in Southside Minneapolis and stays in a house. Her favorite sport is basketball and she wants to be a cosmetologist when she's older.

indig//nant
indig//enous

Matilda Turner

we are the forgotten nation,
an ancestor's lucid dream
we are the southsiders–
where sticks and stones may break our bones
but family can break your heart,
where gunshots mock drum beats,
where sacred was misinterpreted for scared.

this is not the white man's land.
this is our land
our drums pound to mother earth's heart,
this is how gichi-manidoo speaks to us.
he is here. he hears our prayers, our outcries.
we may be made of different pieces
but together we create a masterpiece.

the nation of rebirth and salvation,
the descendants of vitality.
attempted genocide of our people;
they attempt to run us dry
from sick blankets to sterilization
the 'chimook have tried it all.
but alas to no avail, we are still here.
the nation everlasting.

Matilda Turner is a tenth-grade student in the All
Nations program at South High School.

Fortnite Revenge

Tristin Boswell

One time on *Fortnite*, I was put in a game with people who were not speaking English. *Fortnite* is a game that is popular because of how fun it is. They were calling me trash because of my building. I didn't build a big tower like how I could in Playground. Playground is a gamemode that allows players to make whatever they want in the map, like a world or a city with buildings, etc.

So instead, I found a gun that was really powerful and could kill anyone in the game. Then, I won the game for us. After that, they wanted to be my friend. But I blocked them because they were not cool.

Tristin Boswell is a student at South High School. He is in All Nations. He lives near the Riverview Theater with his mom, dad, siblings, and cousin. Tristin enjoys video games and cheeseburgers.

Xbox™ vs. PlayStation™

Daymian P.L.

I feel othered because I have an Xbox One and my friends have PlayStation consoles. Also, I am a better gamer, but they just can't admit it.

The Xbox One has 4K gaming and is extremely better than the garbage PlayStation. The Xbox is also owned by the greatest company in the world, Microsoft. So Sony sees how inferior they are to Microsoft. Sony (knowing they are inferior to Microsoft) then sells their company to Microsoft for $1. Microsoft then discontinues and recalls all PlayStations. With all the money they get from scrapping all the PlayStations, Microsoft gives everyone in the world an Xbox One and everyone lives happily ever after.

P.S. I bought a PlayStation 4.

Daymian P.L. is a student at South High in the All Nations program. He has three cats: Sam, a jet-black cat; Luna, a cat with long gray fur; and Jeff, who is white with large, gray spots. Daymian lives with his mother, two brothers, and two sisters.

Life is normal as normal can be

Tyler Bonete

Sometimes my friends talk about video games I don't play. I feel othered and left out when they talk about some pleb games like *Dark Souls* and *Rainbow Six Siege*, etc.

So to get them to stop, I hire goons to kidnap my friends. I rent a warehouse and bring my friends there and tie them up to chairs with strong rope and I duct-tape their mouths shut. I buy a very powerful speaker system that executes a very loud sound. I put in earplugs and turn on K-pop music on shuffle, which destroys the ears of my friends with its horrible deafening sound. My friends scream in agony, pleading with me to turn the atrocious sound off, and I do so as they comply with my orders. We continue the day watching anime and playing vidya.

Life is normal as normal can be.

Tyler Bonete is a person living on Earth and a student at the All Nations program at South High. He likes pizza. His favorite sport is football.

TYLER

Tyler Bonete

I am from Third Avenue,
from a place with familiar sights.
from a place I've been all my life.

I am a good kid,
I am from the trenches where it's lethal.
I am from where the people live and breathe by
    the Vikings,
where the sports teams let their fans down every
    year.

I am from where they did surgery on a grape.

I am from where there is a constant passing of time
that is slowly bringing us all towards an inevitable
    death.

I Am

Evan Fasthorse

I am from the Southside.
I am Indigenous.

I am from the computer.
I like nothing, nothing, nothing.
I am from Grandma.

I am like the wind.
I like to disappear.
I really don't want to be here.

I think this is stupid,
like President Trump
winning the election.

Evan Fasthorse's favorite thing to do is sleep. And
he has a pet bird. He doesn't know what he wants
to pursue in college.

Zoey B.

Colored pencil on paper
2018

Where I'm From

Zoey B.

I am from Minnesota,
I am Native and white,
Minnesota is like an
Icy island.

Some of my family is enrolled,
From White Earth.
White Earth is quiet and fun,
The only non-quiet part is my family talking.
We talk loud.

The weather is so cold that when you breathe it looks
Like smoke,
Sooo cold your face and hands freeze up.

The city bright,
The sky always lit up,
So many people everywhere.

A lot of events everywhere
Our state can be cold,
But some days it's warm.

Zoey B. is a part of Youth Council. She used to play basketball. She is in ninth grade. Her favorite food is mac and cheese. One of the hardest parts of writing was spelling because I have an IEP because I can't read at my grade level people say, (but I don't give up and I try my best.)

GROWTH

Aniah Smith

Marker on paper
2019

We Are Still Here

Aniah Smith

When I was little I used to get stared at, laughed at, and talked about because I didn't look like I knew how to powwow. I didn't have a pretty bead set with some nice beaded moccasins with nice regalia. Whenever I would go to powwow I didn't know where I fit in. I felt belittled. The girls my age wouldn't let me hang out with them because they looked ready for powwow with their French braided hair, their bead sets, and their full regalia on. Then there was me with my hair braided with a barrette, and with my jingle dress on that was cheaply made because we couldn't afford much.

Little did they know that nobody in my family beaded or sewed, so I had to buy everything I had for powwow. Nobody in my family danced at the time, so I was the one trying to bring that aspect of our tradition back into my family. However, those stares didn't stop me from doing what I loved to do. I pushed through so that I could show them that no matter how unprepared I looked, I knew how to powwow and I knew how to dance. Powwows meant a lot to me at the time, because not only were they one of my coping mechanisms, but that arena was my happy place. The place where I found my peace. The arena isn't just a place to dance—that arena is where you let go of all of your feelings. You feel sad, mad, or stressed about something, you let it out in that arena.

I struggled with letting everything go when people judged me while I danced. I knew I wasn't the best out there, but I knew I was good at it. However, the stares I got, they brought my self-esteem down and made me insecure and scared to dance. That's when I stopped for a while, but not forever. I never made it obvious that I was insecure to dance, but I didn't want to go to powwows anymore, so I didn't. Whenever there would be a powwow I wouldn't go and didn't think anything of it. I stopped dancing around four years ago, and I am now starting to realize the importance of that arena and what it means to me. I want to go back out there and show everyone who laughed at me that I can do what I love without being scared anymore.

I have been practicing and learning how to make pieces of regalia so that when I go back out there into that arena I look ready and I feel ready. When I get back out there I know I will show them that I have changed, that I know more footwork, and that I can compete if I want to. I don't like to compete at powwows because winning money isn't the traditional way, that's not why powwows were made. I like to dance for the culture and not the competition. Powwows mean more to me than just money—they mean tradition to me. We don't have a lot of our traditional ways anymore, and powwowing is a very good way to show people that WE ARE STILL HERE.

I Am

Menewa

I'm from Little Earth,
A place where bad things happen,
Mostly every day.

When I was younger I saw and watched people
    get killed,
Do all different types of drugs,
Get jumped for no reason at all.

And myself,
I have done these things.

And at the time,
I thought it was cool.
Just to be like everyone else.

Looking back,
I regret the things I've done.

I hope someday I can forgive myself.
And I hope the people I've done wrong
can forgive me.

Menewa is a South High student. He lives out in
the 50s with his grandparents. One of his favorite
foods is wild rice.

Lil Durk

JoJo Johnson
Digital illustration
2018

I Was No Saint

jade

Walking into a grocery store you expect to see one thing, food. Now, one thing I wasn't expecting at all to see was a very distressed child and a drained-out mother holding the child's hand. It seemed as if they were about to leave, because I saw the mother holding a single grocery bag ready to go. But the child, who I very quickly learned was named Elena, was holding them back by pointing at an item on the shelf.

Her mother was pulling on the dainty hand lightly, trying to persuade Elena that they were better off going back home and that they didn't need the cereal. The scene in front of me was heartbreaking, and I couldn't help but stand there and watch, amazed by how determined the little girl was to get the cereal.

Wondering if anyone else was seeing the scene that was taking place right in front of me, I began to look around. Some people had walked past them as if they weren't there, while others stole secret glances at the two, judging them with their eyes.

The child kept persuading her mother for the next ten minutes till her mom had had enough and harshly yanked her arm, alarming the little one. "Elena Ruiz, I have had enough! We are leaving now, so put the damn cereal back!" her mother shouted and began walking out of the grocery with her whining daughter right behind her.

I looked around at the people again, seeing what they would do, but nobody did anything. They minded their business and kept walking. I was no saint; I lowered my head and continued walking around the store as if I had seen nothing.

jade is a freshman at All Nations. She has three sisters and one brother and is the oldest of all of them.

Thoughts on the film Dreamkeeper

Skyler Dorr

Pencil on paper

2019

Skyler Dorr is from the Southside of Minneapolis. She stays with her mom, dad, two brothers, two sisters, niece, and nephew. She is a part of the Mille Lacs Band of Ojibwe.

Skyscraper

Michael W.

I am from the Southside.
I am from All Nations.
I am from close friends.
I am from the Ojibwe.

I am as cool as the fall leaves falling from the tree.
I am as tall as a skyscraper is.
I am as Native as a lion is native to Africa.
I am as smart as Albert Einstein.

Michael W. is a student in the All Nations program
at South High School. He lives in a Southside house
with his mom and his dog. Michael's favorite meal is
his grandma's homemade biscuits and gravy.

The Tournament

Joseph Burris

I tried to join the tournament of power. Me, Joey Burris. But I was bad. I had no powers, unlike Goku who has loads. And I was called weak by Yamucha. But when I fell, I had no bruises.

Then, out of nowhere, I saw a UFO. Then I got abducted and the aliens made me fight. I lost and lost but then I met their leader, Jiren the Gray. He laughed and laughed, and to spite him I gained some power. Then I won the tournament of power. Jiren came back and tried to take back the power that was his. I beat all the other aliens, but Jiren was too good and took back his power by absorbing me. In the end, we both had power. :)

Joseph Burris lives with his grandpa and enjoys going to see his cousins on the weekend. He also likes to go to the weight room.

Young Black Elk

Anonymous
Pencil on paper
2018

Black Elk's Spirituality

Anonymous

Black Elk was a spiritual person who lived long ago in the Black Hills. He was born in 1863 and lived until 1950. He was wise about spirituality and the history of his people. He wanted his people to learn about their culture in order to keep their culture alive.

Fire Thunder tells of a battle he fought at age sixteen, the Battle of a Hundred Slain. Black Elk remembers that his father had a limp as a result of the Battle of a Hundred Slain.

Black Elk smoked. His son went to boarding school. He shared his name with his father and grandfather.

He knew that the arrival of white men was not good for his people.

He thought dreams were important, saying, "Sometimes dreams are wiser than waking."

Black Elk had a vision: two men came down from a cloud and said, "Hurry, come to the east, there your grandfathers are calling you."

When the book said, "Black Elk knew that the white people coming would not be comfortable," it was relatable to me because I would feel the same way. During westward expansion and Manifest

Destiny, the white people would have had more stuff, and would have rubbed Black Elk's face in it, and that's how I feel now.

A medicine man named Creeping cured snow blindness by singing a song about the dragonfly. A sacred voice called to Black Elk as a bird who then flew away. A holy man had a dream that poverty was coming.

This student lives in a five-bedroom house. This student lives with five other people and has their own room. Their favorite food is chicken strips with barbeque sauce.

Brave, Curious, Strong, Smart

Brianna P.F.J.

Black Elk is brave, curious, strong, smart. He fought in a battle when he was sixteen and did the buffalo hunt. He wanted justice for his people. Black Elk is relatable because of what he thought. He was related to Crazy Horse. He was a great leader. He had a vision at nine years old: "It was summer and I was nine years old, and our people were moving slowly towards the rocky mountains." Black Elk was special because he had important visions.

I like how inspirational his story has been to our people. He achieved many things in his life. He was victorious in battle. He got many visions from horses and the horse was extremely important. Black Elk says that the horse's voice went all over the universe like a radio and everyone heard it. "It was more beautiful than anyone could be." That is a very powerful statement.

Black Elk's story and visions are here for all of us to get inspiration from and learn from. I still have much to learn. "With this on earth you shall undertake anything and do it." This statement was part of his vision and he takes his vision; he took his visions seriously and did what the spirits said because it was helpful and wise.

Brianna P.F.J. has a cat. She likes to sleep and hang out on Saturdays. She is a part of the All Nations community.

Rayona
Dallas Engen Weiser
Pencil on paper
2018

Dallas Engen Weiser lives in a place called Longfellow.
It is very nice and snowy.

The Beast

Lania Beaulieu

One night my friend and I were walking home.
It was dark and cold. The only lights you could
see were street lights and the phone light on my
friend's face. We were like twenty blocks from her
house and we had a couple shortcuts. We were
both afraid to go through the alleys, but did not
want to express our fear.

My grandma thought I was at her house. My
friend's mom thought we were at the mall with
friends. We had bus cards, but it was so late that
buses weren't out. So we walked past this alley
and we saw something we can never forget. It was
this girl running away from this creature. I could
not take my eyes off it. Suddenly, I found myself
staring in the eyes of the beast.

When the beast grabbed the girl, I knew then he
knew what he was doing. The beast was eating
her, and my friend was on the ground. She had
fallen in fear. I remembered we had a hideout
about a block away! We ran out of there.

We were scared and tired. We did not tell anyone
because we were out too late. We thought if that
girl died, we would hear about it. So . . . we waited
until the next day and heard no word. When we
went back there, we saw blood and the teeth of
the beast. And no body.

45

I can't stop thinking of the beast. As for my friend, she was so insistent on telling, but I talked her out of it because I knew they would send her to the nuthouse, and I would go too because I would back her up.

Lania Beaulieu lives with three cousins, her sister, her mom, her grandparents, and her uncle and aunty. Her favorite way to spend a Saturday is to hang out with friends or be at home watching TV. Lania wants to go to school to become a chef.

Used to be booty, now I'm good

Rey Antonio Saice

I was playing basketball and I didn't get picked because the people I was playing with thought I was booty. But I had to show them how good I was. They made me salty because of that. Then after I didn't get picked, the next game I went to the outhouse 'cause we were on the rez and there were no bathrooms in the gym. But as I was halfway walking, some got-dang ALIENS came outta nowhere and abducted me.

When I was up in their ship, they said they saw me not get picked in basketball and they said they were gonna give me super crossover powers. So when I got back to earth I was trash-talking everybody and I crossed them with my super crossover powers. I shot the ball and I made that ball. And then I went to a tournament that was run by the NBA. The winner would get a contract with the Timberwolves.

But when I was walking home the night before the tournament, I had to walk through a dark area and I just looked up and saw them aliens again and they abducted me again.

They said, "We can't let you keep the powers because you'll become the best ever."

So I was like, "WTH."

And then they dropped me out of the ship and then I went home.

I couldn't sleep all night just wanting to show all them aliens how good I could be without the powers. So that day I went to the tournament really confident. I had to show everybody how good I was.

It was a five-man tournament, so I had to find people to be on my team. I got all the homies. I got Stephan, Trey, Robert, and my brother Joseph. We won the whole tournament and me and all the homies got NBA contracts with the Timberwolves. I had a great career. And then I became the best ever to play basketball. The GOAT. I started from the bottom, now I'm here. Came up from the proj. Used to be booty, now I'm good.

Rey Antonio Saice plays football and also wrestles. Rey's favorite food is bacon.

David Olson

Pencil on paper
2018

David Olson lives with both his parents and three cats.
His favorite sport is basketball.

Alienated

J. Santana

In school, Natives might feel like outsiders in predominantly white schools. At South, the All Nations program seems isolated from the school's Open and Liberal programs. Maybe we're seen as foreign, as if we don't even belong in our own home, due to the lack of interaction. Maybe we need more classes together. But then again, what's the point of the program? The program is focused on Native culture and education.

My solution is there should be more classes together between the programs while still having a balance of classes with a program-specific curriculum. For example, math, science and some electives can be more diverse, whereas social studies or language can be more specific for All Nations only. This would allow us to build a more school-wide community while also having our inner circles.

J. Santana is a sophomore at South High. He lives at his parents' house with two other siblings. He likes to spend his Saturdays hanging out with friends and also enjoys writing because it clears his mind.

FAMILY

J. Santana

Pen on paper
2018

My Family
and Ancestors . . .

Amahpiya Wi

My family and ancestors have pride
My family and ancestors have resisted oppression
My family and ancestors have survived genocide
My family and ancestors have grown into strong
    Native people

Amahpiya Wi means cloud woman in Lakota. In English, this student's name is Ambersky Stevens. She is an enrolled member of the Oneida Nation of Wisconsin. She is also Oglala Lakota, Turtle Mountain Ojibwe, and Menominee. Amahpiya Wi was born and raised in Minneapolis. In the future Amahpiya Wi wants to be a journalist, so she can inform non-Native people about Native issues. Natives have a lot of issues that go unseen, and she wants non-Native people to acknowledge that Natives are still here.

A Family Full of Traditions

Amahpiya Wi

I am from lots of cousins
Who treat me like a sister
From unforgettable memories
From aunties and uncles who care for me like a
    daughter
From the supportive and accepting

I am from Native women, who taught me how to
    be independent
From the strong and loving
From learning everything from my mom and aunties
From the caring and understanding
From women who had to make it without any help
    from a man

Birch Trees

Angelina Deluney

Pencil on paper

2019

Spirit
Angelina Deluney
Pencil on paper
2019

Angelina Deluney is a ninth grade student in the All Nations program at South High School.

Where I'm From

Charles Lyons IV

I'm from a place
Where knowledge is bleak,
Where you looked like a fool,
If you even tried to seek,

Little to none.

This is a place
Where life is as dull as rocks,
Same thing every day,
Just watching clocks,
But now things are a little more interesting,
Now I have a car,
And everything . . .

This is a place where my father went against
    stereotype,
He was there in my life,
But now he's gone . . .

But most people would assume,
He was murdered in the night.
But it wasn't his fault,
He lived almost like a nomad,
Always moving,
He never had a steady home,
My mother told me this sometime after his funeral,
And I wondered, why?

He was perfectly capable of living a great life,
But he chose otherwise.

Ya'know, I had a dream of his passing,
A few days prior,
And I think my aunt had the same dream,
As she was also worried.
She told me to call him,
But younger,
Less caring me
Thought nothing of it,

But now,
I must live with it,
As he lies six feet under,
I'm scared of my dreams now . . .

Charles Lyons IV is a person who is quite fond
of dogs and cats, and his favorite food is noodles,
especially spaghetti. He is also quite fond of Jamba
Juice. He enjoys writing because he can vent via
writing.

Buck Blanket

Mato Ska

Colored pencil on paper

2018

Mato Ska likes lacrosse and is always doing something to mess with other people. He also likes to spend his spare time playing games.

Ghost Dancing/
A Promised Land

Ava Keezer

I am from stories of our elders
From textbooks and history class, a great nation
    we once knew
I am from the stoic Indians, ruthless savages
From crooked and jagged teeth, an animal
A smile not known
I am from enrollment numbers and tribal cards
From a native identified by a piece of paper rather
    than what runs through his veins
Rather than the place his heart comes from
I am from war cries
From Northern Cree powwow songs
Maybe even Fawn Wood if I'm just missing her
I am from grandmother's raising her dough early
    morning
To feed her people
The ones she has left
I am from the arthritis in her hands, she feels that
    storm coming over our people
Wind broken and beaten
From sore and broken feet because all she had
    was church shoes a few sizes too small
Squeezed and crammed into that little space
    meant for us
A trail of tears running down her face
I am from a forbidden tongue

From hands slapped with a ruler if not obeyed
Another game of bloody knuckles, not the one we
    know
From not so holy sermons with a priest
What do they have to confess?
Stories that will shake you to your very core
Hold your grandmother closer to you
A rosary tied around her neck
Yes they stole that from her, a beautiful woman
    she was
I am from a rich land stolen from my people
From greedy little hands searching for a metal to
    calm their little heart's desire
A god's doing
A god's will
I am from dirty water shoved down our throats,
    choking up not saying a word
From oil spills and man camps set up throughout
    a land meant for us
From women being stolen, our men being broken
    and put in a bottle
"Oh yeah I saw about that on TV . . . I thought I
    saw her somewhere—she looked a bit like
    your cousin, didn't she?"
Yes, she was stolen from us, a beautiful woman
    she was
I am from a mother who is in the Creator's world,
    not the one here
Not the one we're in
One I can only dream of
A world she deserves
I am from sitting while this country's song sings
A flag waving genocide and rape

A sickness brought onto us
We still stand
This what our people saw for all of us
Resilience
Don't forget we are from those ghost dances
Bullets flying off our people
Greasy grass and a Hundred Slain
Don't forget we are from our chiefs, our warriors,
    two-spirited people and even medicine men
Can't you hear that?
Can't you hear the jingles, the ribbons on our
    shawls whipping in the wind?
Can't you hear the cries of our people, the treaties
    signed for you and me?
You can't feel that?
Tobacco ties praying for us, praying for our people
    to be strong
A palm on a tree, a sun rising over our people
Suffocated by cigarette smoke, that is not our
    peace pipe
That is not our way
That is not our ceremony
Hasn't our creator told us against the grass you
    smoke? The poison you inject yourself with?
Or is that a pill you're willing to swallow?
Lined up against a wall
We are the seventh generation they envisioned
We will be indigenous strong
We will remain on this land, bones deep rooted in
    the ground
Our bones are here with our people
We remain strong with our ancestors
We remain here with our people

A native nation
A united tribe
Yes, that's my people
Yes, your people
That is where we're from.

Ava Keezer is a tenth-grade student in the All Nations program at South High School.

Where I am from . . .

AnaMaria Tucker

I am from the Southside.
I am from the city rez.
I am from a family with a good sense of humor.
I am from my ancestors.

I am from resilience.
I am from Leech Lake.
I am from the Ojibwe tribe.
I am from my ancestors.

AnaMaria Tucker is a sixteen-year-old girl
who lives in the projects on the Southside of
Minneapolis. Ana lives with her grandma, her
three younger siblings, and her two cats. Ana
wants to pursue a career in nursing. She would
like to be an RN.

Michael W.

Colored pencil on paper
2019

The rez girls are powerful!

Navayah

At my last school, we had to have a partner. So this girl, her skin was way lighter than me. She had to work with me, but she didn't want to.

Then she said out loud, "I don't wanna sit by some rezzy girl."

Shortly after that, an alien came and got her. The alien took control of her mind. She now liked me!

The alien was a protective spirit. She was passed down to me by my ancestors. I guess you could say I inherited her from my mother. I would summon her when I needed an extra hand.

I did not appreciate being called a rezzy girl. It felt negative. The rez girls are powerful!

Navayah has five siblings. She likes to eat french fries. She is a Native American at South High School and she likes dogs.

I am . . .

Gloria Yellow

I am from my dad
  Working hard to make sure the rent's paid
I am from donuts
  I don't like plain donuts
I am from sleeping 'til 10:00 a.m.
  My brothers wake me up from being so loud
I am from money don't grow on trees
  scholarship
I am from the microwave
  Thrown on the floor in a argument
I am from one of my mom's tweaked-out stories
  None of the stories are school appropriate
I am from my grandma's house
  One-bedroom house, the smell of hairspray,
  hangover soup
I am from my brothers
  "Better not have no boyfriend Gloria"

Gloria Yellow is a student at South High School.
She lives two blocks away from the corner
store. She has eight brothers, one sister, and six
nephews and nieces. Her favorite food is Indian
tacos. She wants to be a social worker in the
future and wants to work at Chick-fil-A right now.

Connection to Bravery

Robert Boswell

Ballpoint pen on paper

2018

Robert Boswell is part of the Native community. He lives in a house in Folwell Park with his mom, sister, cousin, and two cats. On Saturdays, Robert enjoys chilling at home.

Space Owl

By GEMINI

His galaxy eyes sparkled,
Watching the river below sparkle.
This was his heaven, his home.
He lifted from the tree, like a rocket.
He soared above the beautiful river,
That belonged to fish and turtles.

The fireflies lit up as he soared against
The bushes below before taking off towards
The lit sky filled with stars.
He was full of pride, this was his home.
Watching the deers make their way
Towards the tall grass.

The wolves howling at the moon,
The pups following along.
He twirled and spun,
He was home. This was his,
His everything, he protected it with his all.
With all the creatures that lived in it,
Small to big, he protected his home.

GEMINI is a 10th grade student in the All Nations
program at South High School.

Truth

Brianna P.F.J.

I am from a broken community,
Where the closest are the ones who tear our hearts.
I am from where people are high up in the clouds,
And can't come back down.
I am from my ancestors.
I am from my "family" that aren't really family.
I am from the Southside.
I am from meeting new people.
I am from doing things I don't want to so I can
    succeed.
I am from mental health issues.
I am from hanging out with friends and being goofy.
I am from the dumba** government.
I am from following rules only when needed.
I am from dishonesty, but also honesty at the
    same time.

Warmth

Daymian P.L.

I am from a place where
Drugs,
Murder,
Theft,
Almost seem legal.

I am from poverty,
and it has consumed everyone and everything.
I am from a place where resources
don't reach people who need them.

I am from love,
Which my mother has given me
By herself.
Love like the warmth of a fire,
A place of
Safety,
Comfort,
Warmth,
And as the embers that come from a fire,
It sometimes hurts.

Seven Grandfather Teachings

Brianna Fair

Felt-tip marker on paper

2018

Never Knew I Was Making Memories

Brianna Fair

I am from where gunshots are my lullaby,
where the booming sounds are what turns the
    lights off.

I am from where fathers never stay long,
Where fathers only bring empty promises.

I am from women yelling,
Men hitting and "Never talk back."

I am from where Spongebob and Mickey Mouse
Were the highlight of my day,
Always wondering what tomorrow would bring.

I am from sitting on the roof when the sun
    disappeared,
And Sandman would come and slip dreams into
    our minds.

I am from where I never knew I was making
    memories.
During my childhood, I was just having fun.

I am from where going outside to the park was the
    most fun
activity you could do before technology took over.

I am from where the people who left me while I
    was young
Always said, "I love you to the moon and beyond
    the stars."

Wonder if they meant what they said.

Brianna Fair is a ninth-grade student in the All
Nations program at South High School.

ABOUT THE SCHOOL

South High School is a public high school that serves nearly 2,000 students in Minneapolis. The school has a tradition of excellence in academic, artistic, and athletic achievement. South has three academic programs: All Nations, Liberal Arts, and Open. All programs provide core programming and preparation for college and opportunities beyond high school.

South is also a school that serves high-needs populations, with rates of free and reduced lunch above 50 percent; 25 percent or more of the student population is classified as English Language Learners.

The students who created this book are from the All Nations program. Designed for American Indian students, yet open to all students, All Nations incorporates resources from the American Indian community to help students graduate in four years and prepare them for a post-secondary education. The program assists students to gain a clear vision of themselves as they develop goals beyond high school. Courses include: Ojibwe language, Native arts, American history from a Native perspective, Native American humanities, and economics/government from a Native perspective.

ABOUT THE PARTNER TEACHERS

Laura Yost Manthey is an English teacher at South High School. After working in Minneapolis Public Schools for thirty years, she acknowledges the rigorous, creative, and sometimes unpredictable demands of teaching as an extreme sport. Her favorite part of teaching in the American Indian community is the compassionate and enlightening intersection where spirituality meets scholarship. As a disciplinarian in the program who makes the best coffee, she truly appreciates the incredible growth students have made in their focus to study and to write. What Yost has learned about herself this year is this: While permissive love may make one popular in the moment, daring to express tough love shapes students for the demands of life.

Audrey Spiess has taught in New York City and Minneapolis Public Schools for the past fifteen years. She has a B.A. in psychology/political science and a master's degree in elementary education. Audrey provides academic support for the students in the All Nations Program at South High in Minneapolis. She has found it to be a privilege to work with the All Nations staff and students. She has never before seen the level of commitment that the staff has for the students. It is a very loving environment. The students are supported with a culturally specific curriculum, and these writing pieces reflect that. Audrey is proud of the students and the work they have done on this project. She feels that her relationships with the students are very valuable and she has learned a lot from them. Audrey considers herself to be an activist, and her work with the All Nations Program aligns with her commitment and passion for the liberation and justice of all people. The indigenous students of South High deserve to be heard.

ABOUT THE ILLUSTRATOR AND DESIGNER

Marlena Myles, Cover Designer and Illustrator

Marlena Myles (Spirit Lake Dakota, Mohegan, Muscogee) is a Native American artist located in St Paul. She uses her art to celebrate her Indigenous culture and language as well as helping the public understand the significance of Native oral traditions and history and their representation through Native art.

She has gained recognition as being one of few Dakota women creating digital art. She hopes her hard work will someday influence other young Native women to enter the art technology field and share their vision with the world. She often works with Native youth in the community, including teaching digital art at the Oscar Howe Summer Art Institute at the University of South Dakota and teaching graphic design to students at Migizi Communications. She also teaches Water Is Life workshops to young Minneapolis students.

Her hope is that the modern tools she uses for her art will be a channel to the youth, to give them the inspiration to create a future that connects with our past, and to create a future that is alive with our cultural values and languages. See her work at marlenamyle.es

Ryan Scheife, Book Designer

Ryan Scheife designs books under the name of his book design company, Mayfly Design, which he has run independently since 2007. He has designed book covers and formatted book interiors for hundreds of publishers and independent authors here in Minneapolis, as well as around the world. His oldest child attends South High and lives in the Longfellow neighborhood. See some of his recent work at mayflydesign.com.

ABOUT MID–CONTINENT OCEANOGRAPHIC INSTITUTE

Mid-Continent Oceanographic Institute (MOI) is a nonprofit organization that empowers underserved K–12 students to think creatively, write effectively, and succeed academically alongside a community of caring volunteers. In a state consistently reporting one of the largest educational opportunity gaps between racial groups in the country, we strive to echo the ethos of the 826 National network by creating a place where no student's idea is too weird, too outlandish, or too off-topic to be explored. We set this accepting tone through our own name and whimsical tutoring space. Our oceanographic branding helps us destigmatize academic support programs, hook volunteers, and promote deep dives into the creative process. MOI seeks to inspire, cultivate, and broadcast students' creativity through the following programs:

After-School Homework Help: This flagship program serves nearly 100 students, K–12, per semester. Hosting four days a week, we pair volunteer tutors one-on-one with students to offer academic support across all subjects.

Storytelling and Bookmaking Field Trips: Available to 2nd–4th grade classes across the Twin Cities, our field trips strive to embolden our next generation of writers to explore and value their own voice. Students and teachers join us to craft original narratives as a class. Volunteers, including an illustrator, work with student authors to publish a book within two hours.

Writers' Room: In our newest program, MOI works in concert with the staff and students at South High School to create a drop-in satellite writing center within the school to support students and teachers for all their writing needs. For teachers this includes lesson plan support and project ideas, and for students this includes help with college essay writing, homework assignments, and even personal writing projects.

Creative Writing Workshops: Each workshop represents a collaboration between student authors, volunteers, and community partners working to create original pieces around a theme.

Young Authors' Book Project: Classroom teachers, volunteers, and MOI staff work together to support students in the creative process of writing original works around a theme. Illustrators, designers, publishers, and printers, many of whom offer their expertise for free, collaborate with students to create a professionally published anthology of their work.

All MOI programs are indebted to the volunteers and community partners who support them. We are honored to be invited into the schools, class-

rooms, and lives of the teachers, families, and students we serve. If you or someone you know has spotted the Lost Ocean of Minnesota, or cares to join us and our students in the search, please find us at www.moi-msp.org.

APPENDIX

EDUCATOR RESOURCES

Our mission at Mid-Continent Oceanographic Institute is to empower K-12 students to think creatively, write effectively, and succeed academically alongside a community of caring volunteers. For this mission to work, for this mission to mean more than just the words on the page, we have to take into account the place and the time that our students live in.

MOI's new headquarters in Minneapolis stands within the most diverse ZIP code in the state of Minnesota. Our neighbors are immigrants and refugees—including families that have only recently arrived and families who have seen their third and fourth generations in the United States. Our neighbors are also Indigenous—including families from the nations that first occupied the Land of 10,000 Lakes, as well as folks representing Native peoples from across the country. These communities are living through a time where elected officials have actively campaigned against their right to exist. They have supported each other and survived through numerous instances of gun violence, police brutality, housing crises and more.

In addition, the current generation of Minnesota schoolchildren has the highest percentage of students of color and Indigenous students in the state's history, and yet only 4 percent of the state's teachers are non-white. Specifically, with our All Nations ninth and tenth graders, we had to confront the historic, oppressive ways the American school system was used as a tool of violence upon Native communities—a trauma which continues to this day. These twin factors, in addition to understanding how our students' environment affects their daily lives, forced our teaching team to deeply consider how and what to ask of our students, when to push them and when to give them space, and why a project like this is both radical and long overdue.

This is where our students come from. They also come from fry bread taco fundraisers, from teachers who will cross snow banks and ice to deliver a sick student their homework, from relatives who continue to stand up and make their voices heard. Despite adversity, this fierce, loving community has exhibited a tremendous and affirming amount of resilience.

In this landscape, MOI came into an urban classroom and asked Indigenous students to write about themselves and be published in a book—this book. Such a feat did not and could not happen overnight. It took months of building trust and understanding, as well as building representation into every lesson plan for the year.

The lesson is not supposed to be the magic wand for racial equity. What follows is an example of just one part of the longer journey that was building a culture of trust in our classroom. We share this knowledge in the hope that more students from historically marginalized communities can see themselves and their stories represented, and through that experience discover their own power.

These materials were inspired by a similar lesson plan from 826CHI, a sister chapter to MOI and part of the 826 National network of youth creative writing and tutoring centers, and developed by MOI's program director Cristeta Boarini based on the high school curriculum of our partner teacher Laura Yost.

LESSON: Change the Ending, Take Back Your Power

3 Sessions, 50 Minutes Each

Goals and Core Curriculum Standards:

- **Literary Analysis:** Determine a central idea of a text and analyze its development over the course of the text, including how it emerges and is shaped and refined by specific details.

- **Creative Writing:** Use literary and narrative techniques such as sensory and descriptive language, hyperbole, and reflection to develop experiences, events, and/or characters.

- **Social/Emotional Learning:** Work in small groups, reflect (for both self and community), and imaginatively problem solve.

Materials: Butcher paper and/or large poster board, markers, and enough copies of short stories for students to read or share.

This lesson simultaneously builds the students' literary vocabulary and their ability to articulate ideas about themselves. These two themes are necessary because the story that this lesson asks them to tell can become both super whimsical and hyper personal.

The lesson starts with an introduction to historical fiction and speculative fiction. This structure worked well for our classes, as they had just started reading the graphic novel version of *Kindred* by

Octavia Butler—a book that deftly combines speculative and historical fiction together.

The final product of the sessions is a short story where the students recount a time they have felt "othered"—discriminated against, left out, or generally made to feel "less than" just for who they are. But then the students have a chance to change the ending in a fantastical way, flipping what was once a hurtful situation on its head.

For many high school students from historically marginalized communities, growing up brings with it a growing understanding of and experience with discrimination—from microaggressions to hate crimes. It is a reality that many students carry with them, but rarely get the opportunity to express. With this lesson they not only get to talk about and release the negativity of those situations, but also get to take back their own power by reimagining a positive outcome instead of the problematic one they experienced.

Before embarking on this lesson, please ensure that you have the staff resources and training to provide an emotionally safe space for students. At South High, we were fortunate to have not only an English teacher with over thirty years of education experience, but also a special education co-teacher and an educational assistant in the classroom every day to support our students and give them the individualized attention that they need. The same MOI staff and volunteers came to each session. In total, we had a consistent team of six staff and volunteers working with about twenty students per class for every session. We rarely had substitutes.

We also had access to our Writers' Room within South High School, which acted as a quieter work space if students needed to work in an environment with fewer stimuli. The work of this lesson plan can be cathartic and healing, but also has the potential to retraumatize a student writer if the proper preparation is not in place.

Session 1: Historical Fiction

Preparation

Building up a familiarity with historical fiction is useful for this activity overall because it helps students see the empowering possibility of countering a dominant narrative. History is told by the victors, but we often find in historical fiction the reimagined voices of history's victims. There is power in a story, especially one of resilience and survival. For students from historically marginalized communities, such stories can be important models for their own lives. This session will also allow students to practice using words about their communities and their lives in relation to storytelling.

Developing word banks (15 mins)

Start the class with four sheets of butcher paper or poster board set around the classroom with markers easily accessible. Each paper should be labeled with one of the following topics:

- Identity

- Culture
- Family
- Community

Divide the class into small groups, with each group starting at a different topic. Encourage the students to write down words that they associate with each topic. These topics should evoke a strong response for students. Allow them to self-identify as much as possible, rather than supplying ideas. There are no wrong answers, but they should be honest answers. After three to four minutes at each station, have the small groups rotate.

Once all the students have rotated through, the lists they have made will likely reveal their values, beliefs, and loves. Many classmates may find similarities that may have been previously unknown or unspoken. It's a simple but energizing activity.

These themes and words associated with them will serve as word banks for the students as they continue to write in this three-part activity. If ever they are stuck or lacking inspiration, direct them to the word banks. The posters can continue to hang around the classroom or may be transcribed into handouts for student reference.

Introduction to historical fiction (20 mins)

Before diving into the short story with your class, take a moment to define historical fiction and to provide context for when the short story the class is about to read takes place. Our class worked with the following historical fiction definition:

Historical fiction imagines how characters might have acted during a historical event or time period. These characters may be invented, or based on real people who existed.

For our classes, we read "They Have Given Us This Land" by Mexican author Juan Rulfo. The story follows a group of farmers in the aftermath of the Mexican Revolution. Another good option would be a Cambodian refugee narrative from the first chapter of *The Clay Marble* by Minfong Ho. Both these examples can be found online for free. Whether you pick these examples or another from your own collection, it is best if the themes or the people depicted in the story are representative of the students in the class. They will have a deeper connection to the material if they can see themselves in it.

Read the short story in small groups. Then, staying in small groups, discuss:

1. Ask the students to share a detail from the story that they related to or that helped them understand it more clearly. Why did this detail stand out to them?

2. What does the story remind them of in terms of community, political, or social issues?

   - For "They Have Given Us This Land," many students identified themes of immigration and deportation, like the migrant caravan of 2018–19, as well as disputed sovereign treaty rights between Native nations and the US government as similar to themes in the story

Writing activity (15 mins)

This prompt will help the students exercise what they have learned. As the class reflects on both the word banks activity and the short story, encourage the students to take on the following writing prompt. They should write at least three to four sentences that utilize some of the words from the word banks. The writing can be on computer, on tablet, or handwritten (depending on what your class has available).

Prompt:

What is the dominant narrative about your ancestors? How has their story been most commonly told over time?

How is that different from what you have been taught by your family? Imagine a moment in history from your ancestors' perspective.

Session 2: Speculative Fiction

Preparation:

Whereas historical fiction helps students see counter perspectives to a dominant narrative, speculative fiction pushes the students to imagine what could be. As the author Simon Sinek has said, "Before we build the world we want to live in, we have to imagine it."

This session will ask the students to push the boundaries of what they know to be possible. Through examples of descriptive, out-of-this-world

texts, they can develop a practice of creative problem-solving that challenges the status quo.

Be sure to have the word banks available for the students again for this lesson.

Introduction to speculative fiction (30 mins)

As with the previous session, take a moment to define speculative fiction before reading the short story. Speculative fiction essentially asks "What if?" What if the world was like X, because of Y reason? Some examples of speculative fiction that students might be familiar with include:

- The Hunger Games: What if we lost a great war, and the punishment was children having to fight to the death?

- *Black Panther*: What if Africa had a secret, technologically advanced kingdom that survived colonialism?

- *Deadpool*: What if you could force someone to develop superpowers by putting them through great stress?

The work of speculative fiction deals with how the characters or society react to those what-ifs.

Like before, have the students read the short story in small groups. In our classes, the students read "Harrison Bergeron" by Kurt Vonnegut. Many were already familiar with the material because they had watched the film version in another class. Other fantastic examples of short speculative fiction include:

- "What Happens When a Man Falls from the Sky" by Lesley Nneka Arimah

- "Childfinder" by Octavia Butler

All these examples can be found online as text or as a podcast.

After reading the short story, have the students discuss the same questions as in the previous lesson. Then encourage the students to compare the stories.

1. Ask the students to share a detail from the story that they related to or that helped them understand it more clearly. Why did this detail stand out to them?

2. What does the story remind them of in terms of community, political, or social issues?

3. Even though one story is set in the past and one is futuristic, what are some similarities? Do the characters face similar struggles? How did they deal with those struggles? Could the resolution in one story work in the other?

Writing activity (20 mins)

Have the students revisit the prompt they started during the last session. Reflecting on the work of the previous prompt and the short stories, encourage the students to answer the following. They should write at least three to four sentences that utilize some of the words from the word banks. As before, the writing can be on a computer, on tablet, or handwritten (depending on what your class has available).

Prompt:

Now, imagine that is 100 years in our future. But this future looks more like our ancestors' time. There is less innovation, less freedom, and fewer resources than we have today. Why is that? What does that feel like? How did it happen?

Allow them fifteen minutes to write, with another five minutes for sharing as a large group.

Session 3: From "othering" to taking back power

Preparation

This is the session where the magic happens. Students and adults alike have expressed how surprised and empowered they were with this prompt. Each part of the session builds on and leads to the overall goal of writing a short story.

During this session, it's important to note that each student may have different definitions and experiences with being "othered." To say to a student, "That is not a good example," would be counterintuitive and harmful. Our teaching team took an approach of "Yes, and..." where we essentially affirmed each student's story and asked them to elaborate on it. This helped the students get to deeper truths while also allowing them to still have ownership of their narratives.

Defining "othering" (10 mins)

At the beginning of the session, have the students write down their definition of feeling "othered." Once they have about five minutes to write their initial thoughts, they can share with the class what their definitions or parts of their definitions are.

After some ideas have been voiced, share with the students a dictionary definition of the term. Merriam-Webster defines othering as "to treat that culture as fundamentally different from another class of individuals, often by emphasizing its apartness."

Take the time to discuss what that definition means and how it applies to the students, breaking down words or phrases as necessary. Our class worked with the simpler definition "to treat someone like they're weird or less than you just because they are different, like because of race or gender, etc."

Reflecting on being othered (20 mins)

With this definition in hand, ask the students to reflect on a time that they might have felt othered. Have them write for about ten to fifteen minutes. Emphasize that there are many different ways that this could happen. Here are some pointers you could give to help the students think:

a.   If they can't think of a time when they felt this personally, maybe it happened to a friend or family member?

b.   It doesn't have to be an issue of discrimination. Maybe they felt left out by friends or siblings.

c. Maybe it wasn't a person, but a system or an organization that did the "othering," like the police, child protection services, or a religious institution.

Be sure to tell the students that they do not have to share this part of their writing with the class at this time. This writing is deeply personal, and potentially holds visceral and traumatizing memories for the students. Let them know that this part is just for them and their reflections.

If you as an educator have a moment of othering to share from your own life, this would be an appropriate time to share it. Be real with the students and model for them the honesty that you hope they could convey in their writing.

Program Director Cristeta Boarini shared with our classes a time she felt othered while working as a journalist. Cristeta is a mixed-race woman, and a person she was interviewing for an unrelated news story demanded to know her ethnicity before continuing the interview. The person then followed the question with a racially ignorant statement.

Many of the students in our class are mixed race and identified with Cristeta's story. Several students stated how they would have responded in such a situation, or they shared that they have had similar questions asked of them. When Cristeta offered herself as an example, the students not only understood the prompt more clearly, but felt like there was an empathetic person in the classroom with them.

As the students wrap up this portion of the writing, vocally thank and commend them for doing the work. This writing takes a huge effort, and it's important as an educator to show your appreciation that the students were willing to put themselves out there. Acknowledge that it can be really hard to write about a time when you felt powerless, but it can also be a release.

Change the ending, take back your power (20 mins)

At this point, the students will have a chance to change the ending of their "othering" story. The students should be encouraged to change the ending in a way that makes them feel powerful, especially to do so in a fantastical way. By "fantastical," we mean making the seemingly impossible, possible. Dragons, aliens, spirits, super powers, high fantasy, campy horror—are all fair game.

As you introduce the concept of changing the ending of their stories, students should be encouraged to draw from the short stories they read in earlier sessions for inspiration. This is also a good opportunity to remind the students to utilize the word banks from the first session to find the words to tell their story. Recall for the students what they learned in the historical and speculative fiction lessons. What were the power dynamics of those stories? What details and literary devices did the author add to help readers understand those power dynamics? These can be helpful questions as they think about changing the ending.

Chicago writer Eve Ewing has many examples of this type of story—a genre she calls [retelling] in

her 2017 book *Electric Arches*. Her characters gain the ability to fly or become possessed by spirits as consequences of an "othering" interaction. Ewing's stories are short, and offer a strong model for the class to follow. The book is available on Amazon if you cannot find it in your local bookstore.

In *Indigenous Originated: Walking in Two Worlds*, "Used to be booty, now I'm good" by Rey Antonio Saice is a perfect example of the prompt. Rey recounts a moment many of us can relate to: not getting picked for a basketball team. He then switches the power dynamic with the help of some aliens and his best friends.

Our classes were told to avoid violence in their new endings. Instead, the students were encouraged "to be more creative than that," and we redirected them to other whimsical possibilities. This feedback was received positively.

There will be laughter and there will be reticence as you and your students go through this exercise. But with patience, the work they create can grow to be incredibly profound. As time allows and as your students need, additional sessions can be held for continued writing, editing, revising, or peer review. Our classes' additional sessions included time to revise, illustrate, and add literary devices like hyperbole, local color, and cause and effect to their stories.

You can find more resources like this on our website, www.moi-msp.org, or through 826 Digital, an online collection of lesson plans and resources created by the 826 National network of creative writing and tutoring centers.